The Life of Chesterton

The Life of Chesterton

THE MAN WHO CARRIED A
Swordstick AND A *Pen*

Holly Geiger Lee

Illustrated by
Nellie Buchanan

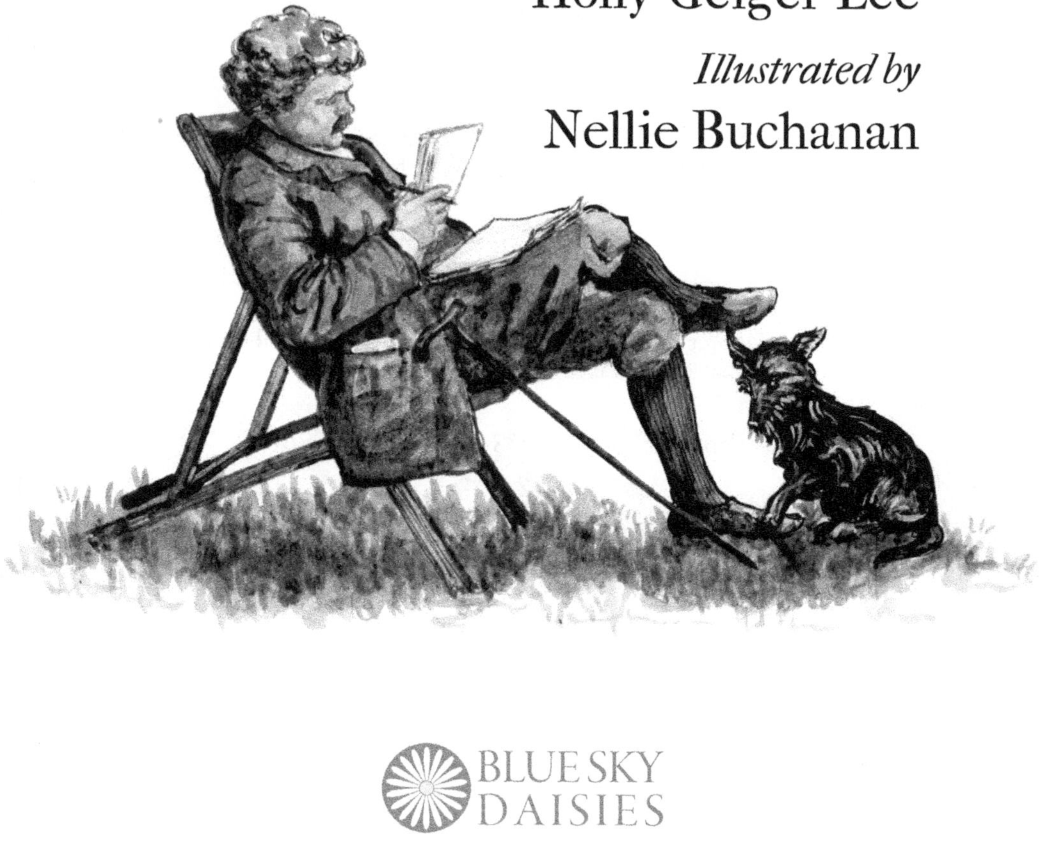

BLUE SKY
DAISIES

The Life of Chesterton: The Man Who Carried a Swordstick and a Pen
By Holly Geiger Lee © 2024
Illustrations by Nellie Buchanan © 2024

Blue Sky Daisies
Wichita, Kansas

Cover Painting by Nellie Buchanan © 2024
Cover Design © Blue Sky Daisies

All Rights Reserved. No part of this book may be used or reproduced in any manner whatsoever without written permission.

Scripture quotations from the King James Version.

This biography is a work of creative non-fiction for young readers; some dialogue and descriptions are imagined for narrative purposes and are not meant to be direct quotations. Direct quotations are credited at the conclusion of this book.

Paperback ISBN: 978-1-944435-44-8

For
Andrew, Nathanael, Virginia, and Connor
– H. G. L.

To
my brother Will,
for introducing me to so many beautiful things in life,
not the least of which were
the writings of G. K. Chesterton.
– N. B.

Contents

MAP OF CHESTERTON'S ENGLAND • 9

1. The Very Beginning • 11
2. Boyhood and Imagination • 21
3. School Days and Friendship • 35
4. Art School and Darkness • 43
5. Gratitude and the Light • 51
6. Mrs. Chesterton • 59
7. Man of Ideas • 77
8. Joy and Suffering • 89
9. Patience • 101
10. Stepping out into the Light • 113

AUTHOR'S NOTE • 117
REFERENCES • 119
ACKNOWLEDGEMENTS • 121
ENDNOTES • 122

Map of Chesterton's England

Chapter One

The Very Beginning

One autumn day in 1925, a man sat writing outside Market Harborough Railway Station. Whatever he was writing must have been amusing, because he suddenly burst into laughter. His laughter echoed against the red brick railway station building.

The man looked up from the stack of papers on his knee that would become his next book and began to stand up. He kept rising up and up, higher and higher above the platform, until he reached his full height of six feet, four inches. His signature cape was a faded gray, and his crumpled velvet hat was a midnight black.

Gilbert Keith Chesterton was anything but typical.

Always overflowing with ideas, the tall, portly man awaiting a train was well-known to his fellow Englishmen, who loved to attend his lectures and read his newspaper articles and books. He was a lover of what he called "little England." Gilbert was inspired by an English king of old who had lived in Wessex nearly 1,000 years prior. The king, named Alfred, had had to defend his part of England from Viking invaders. King Alfred the Great had fought to protect what he had held dear: his countrymen and his culture. And like King Alfred the Great, this man was also an intellectual, a thinker, and a defender. He was a defender of truth and tradition.

When Gilbert took a stand against something, he stood firmly. However, he did it with a great respect for the opposing side.

He was a man of generous girth, weighing about 300 pounds. Swordstick in hand, cigar in mouth, and tiny glasses pinched to the tip of his nose, he put his entire body into a laugh that sang through his mustache, as he was suddenly jolted by the reality of having missed his train and having no idea whatsoever where he had been heading.

"Where on Earth am I supposed to be?"

He puzzled. He pondered. Then, he shrugged.

Minimally flustered, he made his way over to the railway ticket office to telegraph his wife. Writing down a message, he handed a slip of paper to the operator.

It read: "Am at Market Harborough. Where ought I to be?"

He decided to sit on the platform bench as he awaited his wife's reply. Gilbert looked to his right, then up, gazing at the rail bridge. The bridge triggered a vivid memory. A long train of memories began moving through his mind, like train cars following along behind an engine.

Gilbert Keith (G. K.) Chesterton thought of his first and favorite memory—the memory of his father's toy theater.

When Queen Victoria was still on the throne, little Gilbert had gazed eye-level at a toy theater that his father, a man of a hundred hobbies, had crafted. He had looked at a tiny man walking across a bridge in the theater's scene. The miniature man had a curly mustache, and to young Gilbert he seemed to swagger as he walked. His hand held a disproportionately large, golden key. Atop his head rested a shiny, gilded crown.

From his bench at the train station, Gilbert followed the passersby with his eyes, but his mind was back in his father's study, fondly thinking about that enchanting man on the toy theater's bridge. Where was that crowned man looking? At a tall castle tower. There within the castle's single window was a young lady, gazing back at the prince on the bridge. Between the bridge and the princess in the tower, there was a deep valley, all made in miniature in his father's little toy theater.

Gilbert liked to say that anything in childhood was a wonder. "Not merely a world full of miracles; it was a miraculous world." Even the ordinary was extraordinary for children.

He also remembered the walks he had taken with his mother as a small boy. They would stop for a glass of milk at a dairy that had a figure of a white cow in front. That

He decided to sit on the platform bench as he awaited his wife's reply.

enormous white cow seemed magical to him. He also loved the paint shop next door. The one with gold paint and pointed, colorful chalks.

He remembered back to when the red houses on the hill near Holland Park were new. From their terraces one could look toward London, off in the distance, and spy the sunlight sparkling off the iron and glass of the Crystal Palace.

Sitting there at Market Harborough, Gilbert smiled to himself about the toy theater. The white cow at the dairy. The paint shop. The sparkle of the Crystal Palace. And the painted, white hobby-horse. He couldn't remember the particulars of the hobby-horse now. Where was he when the light streamed into a room as he watched someone painting a hobby-horse head with milky white paint? He didn't know anymore. But it was a happy memory.

Gilbert Chesterton was born on the 29th of May in 1874, fifty-one years before that day at the railway station. As a child, Gilbert was affectionately called "Diddie" by close family and friends. Diddie spent many a day in his family's London neighborhood, fighting pirates and frolicking among the jasmine, iris, and roses outside their home at 11 Warwick Gardens. Wisteria blossoms crept along the exterior walls of the brick and stucco homes on his street. The warm air smelled of roses. Kensington was abuzz with the sights and sounds of spring. There he galloped about on his hobby-horse, taking a stick and using it as a sword to fend off the fast-approaching pirates. His five-year-old imagination made the pirate ship appear on the rollicking waves of his mother's boxwood bushes.

The blue sky made a perfect backdrop for the maritime battle. Sunlight reflected off his blonde hair. His mother's dark green window boxes held flowers that morphed into onlookers as he fought the pirates. *Swish!* The sword cut through the air, barely missing the neck of the nastiest-looking pirate of them all. How much fun it was to play!

Upon entering the rose-colored drawing room of their home, Diddie was greeted by his mother who looked a little bit like himself. She had her clothes thrown on in an untidy fashion. Looking around for her misplaced cup of tea, she heaved a heavy sigh and collapsed into a deep, velvet chair. She was incredibly tired, and rightly so. Marie-Louise

"There you are, Diddie, darling! How was the sunshine?"

Chesterton was pregnant, expecting a new brother or sister for Diddie.

"There you are, Diddie, darling! How was the sunshine?"

"Oh, Mother, the usual pirates came back to fight! You need not worry. I got them," the small boy beamed.

"Splendid! I know how you fancy fighting off pirates," Marie-Louise smiled at her imaginative son.

As she looked at Gilbert, perhaps Mrs. Chesterton wistfully remembered her first child, Beatrice, who had been only eight years old when she died. Diddie had been three years old when it happened, and he barely remembered his sister, whom the family had affectionately nicknamed "Birdie." The nicknames Diddie and Birdie most likely had come from Gilbert's own faulty pronunciation of the names as a youngster.

After Birdie died, each member of the family had grieved in a different way. Gilbert's mother had mentioned Birdie to a family friend once. "I *was* the mother of three children," she had said, "and I had a beautiful girl." On the other hand, his father refused to even speak of sickness and even ignored his own heart condition. If Diddie or anyone else were to fall ill, Edward Chesterton would ignore it, wishing it away by looking away. He was never able to speak his daughter's name again, preferring to put aside those emotions.

Marie-Louise looked over at her son, disheveled from play, and affectionately stroked his cheek. She placed her hand on her own round belly and felt a kick from the baby. "This baby will bring a lot of happiness and hope back to the family," she thought to herself.

Gilbert took in the surroundings of the drawing room. He felt comforted by its rose-colored walls. To him, the color rose meant home and family. Although the Chestertons had known sorrow, they were a loving and happy family. Diddie loved his childhood.

The world was full of miracles. Indeed, it was miraculous.

Chapter Two

Boyhood and Imagination

For Gilbert, the miraculous world was marked by Shakespeare's verse, George MacDonald's fairy tales, poems of ancient Rome, and delightful rhymes by W. S. Gilbert—all experienced from the comfort of his middle-class Victorian home's velvet, wood, and leather furnishings. His father, whom family and friends called "Mr. Ed," loved to tinker. Not only did he build an enchanting toy theater, he filled his study with all manner of projects. He was interested in photography, watercolor painting, medieval illumination (bright and colorful paintings adorning the calligraphy of manuscripts), and stained glass. He often hung fairy-lamps in the garden on special occasions, transforming its flowers and trees into a magical place.

"What are you making this time?" G. K. asked Mr. Ed, who stood hunched over the latest set he was making for the toy theater. This one would become a colorful seaside holiday scene. The intricate waves, beachgoers, and beach tents he was painting on each panel reminded G. K. of happy holidays. Once Mr. Ed was finished painting the panels, he would attach the theater floor piece to the walls that framed the stage. Next, he would make incisions in the theater floor and would slide a proscenium arch into the slits. This proscenium arch would create an authentic effect. When he had finished gluing the pieces together, he would make the figures of the characters. Once he finished this, he and his family would entertain guests with their own imaginative plays and comedies. At the moment, he was working on the figure of a large boat.

"My dear boy, I am arranging this frigate into the scene. See the tall masts and the white sails? How does it look?" Mr. Ed exhaled and stepped back for a moment to inspect. He waited for his son's reply.

"I do love it! You do the best work. It reminds me of Ariel's song:

>Come unto these yellow sands,
>   And then take hands;
>Court'sied when you have, and kiss'd,—
>   The wild waves whist—"

"My boy! Your mind is as sharp as a nail!" Mr. Ed exclaimed and burst into jolly laughter at Gilbert's quoting the lines from *The Tempest*. He patted G. K. on the shoulder.

"But have you memorized *King Lear*? I will teach it to you one day in its entirety. Such a tragedy! However, one of Shakespeare's supreme achievements, my lad. Oh, you'll love it!"

G. K. loved his father and his father's love for English literature. Edward Chesterton was carrying on the family real estate business as a house agent, but a variety of subjects fascinated him. He was more than a house agent; he was a toy theater architect, artist, and avid reader.

"You're always so merry! Have you ever been glum?" G. K. wondered aloud.

"Life, family, and laughter, Gilbert. These things are what make me so merry. There is simply no time to be glum!" Mr. Ed's kind eyes gazed upon his son's blonde mop of hair. No matter what G. K. ended up doing in life, Edward would always adore that boy. Little Gilbert thought that there could be no greater parents in the world. How exciting it was that he would be getting a new baby brother or sister!

School was often a bore for G. K., as he did not like formal instruction interrupting his thoughts or hobbies. Before he grew big enough to attend school, Gilbert learned the Greek capital letters just for fun. They were charming and mysterious to him. He could always recognize the Greek letter *theta* because it looked like Saturn and his rings, and *upsilon* stood tall like a curved chalice. But when he was sent to school and made to learn the lower-case Greek letters in his lessons, Gilbert thought they looked like a swarm of nasty gnats. Where was the charm in that?

Gilbert wanted to explore all sorts of things he was curious about, and school lessons seemed only to get in the way of his discoveries. Books lined the walls of the Chesterton home in Kensington and took him on journeys into distant times and places. George MacDonald's fairy stories ignited the flame of his imagination. Oh, how he loved MacDonald's tale, *The Princess and the Goblin*. It was one of his favorites. The ordinary rooms and halls of his home were transformed into magical places as Princess Irene explored the cavernous castle and came upon her great-great-grandmother, who gave her a magical ring. Behind this ring trailed an invisible thread, tethering Irene constantly to home. With evil goblins lurking in the nearby mines and tunneling under the castle, Irene found help from Curdie, a young miner. Every time Gilbert read the story, he felt as if he were there in the thick darkness of the mines with Curdie and Irene, sharing their adventure. The power of MacDonald's words had a strong effect on Gilbert. He later said that MacDonald's fairy tale formed his moral understanding of the threat of evil—evil inside, not outside.

Thomas Babington Macaulay's *Lays of Ancient Rome* was another favorite of his. The emerald green book had a beautiful gold, embossed illustration of Horatius standing heroically, shield in one hand, sword in the other, with his foot planted triumphantly upon his fallen foe. Pulling the book down from the shelves, Gilbert often plopped down on the floor with the *Lays* before him and opened it to the beloved ballad *Horatius*. With a horde of enemy soldiers approaching the bridge and sure to overwhelm their town, brave Horatius declares,

> I, with two more to help me,
>   Will hold the foe in play.
> In yon strait path a thousand
>   May well be stopped by three.

> Now who will stand on either hand,
>   And keep the bridge with me?

Gilbert never tired of reading the tale of Horatius's glory. "Oh, to be so brave and bold!" Gilbert said aloud, as he read the lines,

> And wives still pray to Juno
>   For boys with hearts as bold
> As his who kept the bridge so well
>   In the brave days of old.

G. K. was especially fond of a book his father had made but never published, full of pictures drawn by Mr. Ed of old Dutch houses. Gilbert loved to study the pictures and imagine what was unseen. What might be hiding in the side streets of the quaint, little town? What was around the corner and not visible in the picture? He imagined all sorts of things.

After his mother gave birth to his little brother Cecil in 1879, it was said that Gilbert announced, "Now I shall always have an audience!" But the truth was that when

*Edmund Clerihew Bentley was a young stranger to Gilbert.
That was about to change!*

Cecil grew out of babyhood, the two boys argued constantly. Gilbert never shied away from discussion with Cecil, because it was a chance to engage someone in conversation. He loved conversation!

One day when Gilbert was probably eleven or twelve years of age, he met a new friend on the playground of Samuel Bewsher's preparatory school (later named Colet House). Edmund Clerihew Bentley was a young stranger to Gilbert. That was about to change! Edmund came charging at him out of nowhere. The two boys started wrestling, "rushing hither and thither about the field and rolling over and over in the mud," a deep, insatiable impulse to wrestle welling up in each of them. There was nothing vindictive in the exchange, for the two had never met before, after all.

"Just what do you think you're doing? Are you trying to pick a fight with me?" G. K. gasped for air as he struggled to keep up with Edmund's quick sprint.

Both boys knew their fight was all in jest.

"You rascal!" Gilbert wheezed.

"You'll never catch me!" the boy jabbed.

With a flying leap, G. K. bounded towards his adversary, and the two boys found themselves rolling over and over one another in the mud. It was a good-natured tussle, and it lasted for almost an hour. (Nobody was keeping time, really.)

So, how did it end? Stopping for a quick breath, Edmund began reciting with a rollicking cadence.

> "The other night, from cares exempt,
> I slept—and what d'you think I dreamt?
> I dreamt that somehow I had come
> To dwell in Topsy-Turveydom!
>
> Where vice is virtue—virtue, vice:
> Where nice is nasty—nasty, nice
> Where right is wrong and wrong is right—
> Where white is black and black is white."

G. K. immediately recognized his words. "Oh! the *Bab Ballads* by W. S. Gilbert! You're reciting the beginning of one called 'My Dream.' My father used to say it to me. Such irony, where everything that's true is not true. All the right seems wrong and the wrong seems right. Did you have the book?" G. K. huffed and puffed, now eagerly engaged in deep conversation.

"My mother loves W. S. Gilbert. She recited this one to me nearly every day when I was a lad. It stuck, didn't it? One day, I'd like to attend one of the Gilbert and Sullivan comic operas! My mother goes on and on about the dancing, the music, the dialogue. She saw *The Mikado* at the Savoy Theatre." Edmund smiled.

"Do you mean the Savoy where they just installed all of those new-fangled lamps that run on electricity? It's the first public building in the world to be lit by electricity! No more gas lamps—can you believe it?" G. K. marveled.

Gilbert loved scribbling pictures to go with Bentley's rhymes.

When Gilbert quoted from Macaulay's *Lays*, and Edmund finished the lines, the two boys fell into a lively and long conversation about their favorite books. A knowing nod and swift nudge marked the beginning of a lifelong friendship.

Gilbert and Edmund, whom Gilbert called by his surname Bentley, were both steadily leaving childhood behind and entering the more grown-up world of schoolboys.

"Boyhood," Gilbert said later, "is a most complex and incomprehensible thing. Even when one has been through it, one does not understand what it was." G. K. saw a distinct difference between children and schoolboys. He liked to say that schoolboys everywhere tended to hang out in threes, wander around to no where in particular, and suddenly break into a fight—only to stop just as suddenly.

It wasn't that schoolboys quit pretending. Gilbert and his friends loved to pretend. But children say, "Let's pretend we're Vikings!" Schoolboys no longer announce their intention—they just pretend. And when they do, whether they be Vikings or pirates, what they are truly doing is pretending to be men.

When Gilbert was fourteen, he sent Bentley a letter. The boys were planning a tableaux, a sort of costume drama, including "among others King John signing the Magna Carta, Dream of Richard III, St. George and the Dragon, etc."

Gilbert signed the letter:

I am,
Your grovelling serf, villein and vassal,
G. K. Chesterton

The boys had great fun together, never lacking for adventure. Gilbert later said the worst thing that can happen to a schoolboy is to be reminded that he is not, in fact, an independent gentlemen, all grown-up. Schoolboys loathe any mention of parents or siblings because this shatters their secret agreement of pretending together that they are grown gentlemen of means. Maybe formal education was a bore, but school friends made school days an adventure.

Bentley had extraordinarily well-balanced brains and could do almost anything with them. He was of the variety that could stock a library with his wit and literary rhymes.

For Bentley, chemistry class was not just chemistry. If you had passed by his desk and happened to snatch up his blotting paper, what do you think you would have seen on the page? Perhaps you would have expected to see a chemical equation or the periodic table of elements. If you had looked a little closer, here is what you would have read:

> Sir Humphrey Davy
> Detested gravy.
> He incurred the odium
> Of discovering sodium.

And who would you expect had drawn the sketches to accompany these quirky verses? Gilbert loved scribbling pictures to go with Bentley's rhymes.

"Boys," Gilbert said, "wander in threes." Gilbert and Bentley made a trio with their friend Lucian Oldershaw. The three of them were regular Three Musketeers. It never occured to them in their school days that all three would grow up to become well-known, published writers. But even as G. K. grew up and left his boyhood behind him, he never left behind his imagination.

Chapter Three

School Days and Friendship

Having finished preparatory school at about the age of twelve, the three friends entered St. Paul's, a distinguished day school in Hammersmith. The recently built red-brick and terracotta building of St. Paul's was situated along Hammersmith Road, not far from Gilbert's home neighborhood of Kensington.

In his early years at St. Paul's, Gilbert's genius went unnoticed by his teachers. He often seemed to be daydreaming—asleep, even—and not paying attention. But his mind was busy, always occupied with thinking or dreaming.

More than ever, he read books. Shakespeare's plays and poems; George MacDonald's fairy tales and essays; Dickens' *Pickwick Papers*; the Victorian-era poetry of Alfred, Lord Tennyson and Robert Browning; Sir Walter Scott's *Ivanhoe*; John Milton's *Paradise Lost*; Dante's *Comedy*.

When Gilbert was sixteen, Lucian Oldershaw proposed that they form a club. Their first official meeting took place at Lucian's house. Gilbert, Bentley, and Lucian gathered together with nine other friends and elected officers for their newly named Junior Debating Club (J. D. C.). Gilbert was elected chairman; Lucian was secretary.

They felt important and wrote out the club's purpose and rules. The J. D. C. would gather together to discuss any literary subject they took an interest in debating. Each member had to write regular literary papers. Absent twice in a row? Fined sixpence. Unwilling to read your paper aloud to the group? Fined sixpence. None of this spoiled the fun. On the contrary, they held lively debates, and the teenage boys must surely have felt like grown men.

They agreed on a motto: "Hence loathed Melancholy." It was a line from John Milton's poem *L'Allegro* (which is Italian for "The Happy Man"). The members of the J. D. C. were committed to good cheer and happiness.

Oh, the memories they had together! They met at each others' homes after school or on Saturdays. On the day of a club meeting as the school day would draw to a close,

. . . a sticky bun was launched, soaring across a vast field of papers and stinging the cheek of its unsuspecting victim, the chairman Chesterton.

the dozen club members anticipated the head porter's bell.

BONNNGGG!

They were off! The J. D. C. members took off running, this time headed for 11 Warwick Gardens. Upon entering Gilbert's home, they removed their cloaks and hats and settled into velvet armchairs or high-backed dining chairs arranged before a chalkboard filled to the brim with ideas. Mrs. Chesterton greeted them as she usually did, "Hello, Bentley, darling! Do come in, Oldershaw, darling!" She brought copious pots of hot Darjeeling tea to be served. Sticky buns made their way around the circle of young gentlemen, which they hastily devoured. Gilbert's younger brother Cecil would join them, although he wasn't as popular with his friends as his father and mother were.

Once, during a rousing debate, a sticky bun was launched, soaring across a vast field of papers and stinging the cheek of its unsuspecting victim, the chairman Chesterton. The young men erupted in uproarious laughter which continued for minutes thereafter.

Lucian had a new idea. Why not publish a magazine?

Throughout their time at St. Paul's, they would publish *The Debater* eighteen times. They wrote all the articles, arranged for typesetting and printing, and sold copies of their new publication. The members of the J. D. C. were delighted when the first issue sold out. Gilbert was astonished that they had accomplished it. He remembered it later,

They wrote all the articles, arranged for typesetting and printing, and sold copies of their new publication.

Our debating club was actually founded and did actually debate, if it can be called debating. This part of the matter did not alarm me much; for I had debated off and on ever since I was born; certainly with my brother, probably with my nurse. But, what was infinitely more bloodcurdling, our paper did actually appear in print.

It was a triumph for the club, and their teachers began to

notice. They wrote on a variety of topics, sometimes writing about great authors and their works. But sometimes their subjects were more whimsical. Gilbert contributed a piece called "Dragons" to the very first issue.

> The dragon is certainly the most cosmopolitan of impossibilities. His eccentric figure has walked through the romances of all ages and of all nations . . . apparently with the sole object of being killed, whether by the lance of St. George, the club of Herakles, the sword of Siegfried, or the arrows of Hiawatha.

G. K. Chesterton's writing was already memorable at age sixteen.

This group of thinking young men formed a culture in and of itself. In fact, in the J. D. C., Gilbert found a sort of intellectual apprenticeship. He encountered plenty of ideas to mull over, plenty of good authors to read, and plenty of opportunities to share one's own ponderings with other eager listeners. The group of friends continued to grow and thrive, as they shared their love of ideas, good literature, and good tea.

During his time in the J. D. C., Gilbert received the Milton Prize for a poem. He later remarked with his typical self-deprecating humor,

> I imagine it was about as bad as all other prize poems, but I am happy to say that I cannot recall a single syllable of it.

Before he had found his friends, G. K. described himself as "solitary; not sorry, but solitary." How that had changed for him in just a few years! On his seventeenth birthday, the club's secretary, Lucian Oldershaw, stood up and announced loudly, "Here! Here! It is the anniversary of our esteemed chairman's Natal Day! I propose a vote to wish him 'Many Happy Returns!'"

They sang their club song with gusto.

> *I'm a Member, I'm a Member, Member of the J. D. C.*
> *I'll belong to it for ever,*
> *Don't you wish that you were me?*
> *Then pass the cup, debaters all*
> *And fill the tea-pot high,*
> *And o'er the joy of wild debate*
> *May hours like moments fly.*
> *As critics quiet and composed,*
> *As brothers kind and free,*
> *Join hand in hand the tea-pot round,*
> *Joy to the J. D. C.!*

Gilbert fondly remembered his years at St. Paul's. His instructors and fellow students remembered him as well. When his mother spoke with the headmaster about Gilbert's future, he told her, "Six feet of genius. Cherish him, Mrs. Chesterton, cherish him." Little did Gilbert know that his world was about to turn upside down.

Chapter Four

Art School and Darkness

Schoolboys no more, the men of the J. D. C. had completed their time at St. Paul's, and most of them left London for Cambridge or Oxford to begin their university education. But not Gilbert. Mr. Ed had encouraged his son to attend art school, and the University College in London's Slade School of Art offered the latest modern education in art. Perhaps Gilbert's father was wistfully wishing his son could pursue art in a way that he had never been able to, but Gilbert himself was already devoted to drawing at the time, and art school seemed like a natural choice.

Gilbert kept in touch with Bentley and Oldershaw especially. Bentley often sent him letters, filling him in on life at Oxford. When he wrote about the new club they were forming, Gilbert felt a twinge of jealousy. Like the J. D. C., the new club would be focused around discussion and reading papers to each other. Bentley described to Gilbert their trouble picking a name for the new club. One friend liked "The Whitmen," a clever play on words with "wit" and Walt Whitman, the poet they all admired. But they had dismissed it as sounding too exclusive. Oldershaw wanted to call it "The S. U. (Some of Us)" or, his other suggestion, "The Hugger Mugger Club." A hugger-mugger was either someone keeping secrets, or someone in a disorganized mess. Bentley thought "Tinkling Symbols," more clever word play (as the apostle Paul had written that those without love were "tinkling cymbals"). In the end, the group called themselves the Human Club.

Wallowing a little in his loneliness, Gilbert wrote this poem:

An Idyll

Tea is made; the red fogs shut round the
    house but the gas burns.
I wish I had at this moment round the table
A company of fine people.
Two of them are at Oxford and one in
    Scotland and two at other places.
But I wish they would all walk in now, for
    the tea is made.

Art School and Darkness

G. K. found himself descending into a dark night of the soul. Art school created an unusual environment. It was hard to learn to paint! G. K. looked around him and expected to see all the other art students laboring to make their paintings just right. Yet, it seemed as though most of the students in his class could not have cared less about learning to paint well. Art school was a place where a few people in the school worked with feverish energy, while all the others idled the days away. Many of the students whiled their time away in groups, chatting and complaining. Meanwhile, the professors at Slade were excited about the latest movement in fine arts, Impressionism.

The Impressionist movement in art was new, radical, and taking Europe by storm. This movement took painters out of the studio to the outdoors to paint scenes of life and nature. Painters used heavy daubs of paint to depict scenes not necessarily as they *appeared*, but as the artists *perceived* them. They wanted to represent on their canvases what the landscapes made them *feel* rather than record an exact representation of what they saw with the eye. Painters were interested in creating an *impression* of the scene, not a photograph-like painting.

G. K. sat in class as his art teacher described how to paint a cow. "Now, I start with a white line and a purple shadow. You see how my brush evokes this perception of a cow? I feel it is a cow. So, it must be a cow! You see, students? This is the real beauty of Impressionism! It seems as if it is real—you perceive it to be real, so it must be real. Let it be whatever you perceive it to be."

His teacher had become so enthusiastic about his subject matter that beads of sweat started to appear upon his face. He appeared so zealous that he almost seemed crazy.

"It's a white line and a purple shadow," G. K. thought to himself. He furrowed his brow. He looked harder. "I still see a white line and a purple shadow. I do not see a cow. Teach me how to paint a real cow!" He frowned some more.

G. K. was discouraged. If things were truly only what he perceived them to be, did things really exist at all? He sighed. These ideas were dangerous. If true, it meant that nothing was real. Nothing mattered. Nothing had meaning. Confronted with these thoughts, Gilbert's mind plunged into an abyss of darkness.

His despair was evident in his drawings. G. K. found himself sketching devilish images in a notebook as he plunged deeper and deeper into a pit of spiritual despair. Gilbert kept on scribbling in his notebook. His pen scribbled away as if that might help rid his mind of the unwelcome ideas. One day, two of his friends discovered one of the notebooks with the dark drawings. They rightly asked, "Is Chesterton going mad?" He wasn't mad, but as Gilbert later said, "I was simply carrying the skepticism of my time as far as it would go."

What about Horatius's noble deeds to save his town?

"I feel it is a cow. So, it must be a cow!"

Did bravery and self-sacrifice amount to nothing? G. K. wrestled with the new ideas, but he just couldn't accept them. There *are* goblins under the castle! Evil *is* real, and people ought to fight against it as bravely as Horatius fought the enemy soldiers to the last.

Gilbert's family was not particularly religious and rarely spoke of a personal God. Gilbert described himself as agnostic, not really knowing if a personal God existed. But as he struggled with despair, he thought back to the white horse in his nursery, and the light shining across it. Why was Gilbert now stumbling without hope in a dark, murky forest? Why was the dark hard to distinguish from the light?

He seemed to be in a dark wood, searching for the sun or moon, but all he could find were the shadows cast by the light. These shadows made it hard to discern to which shapes they belonged. What was G. K. seeing? He wandered some more through the forest of his mind. The path suddenly vanished. All of a sudden, there was no path or gate leading out. There were only shadows and woodland mist.

"What is my purpose? Why am I alive?"

Years later, he described the darkness of the modern, meaningless philosophies in a poem which he dedicated

G. K. found himself sketching devilish images in a notebook.

to his life-long friend Bentley, comparing the disturbing ideas to a sick cloud in a few of the lines.

> A cloud was on the minds of men,
> and wailing went the weather,
> Yea, a sick cloud upon the soul
> when we were boys together.

But he could see in hindsight that he and Bentley were not overcome by the darkness around them. Later in the poem he wrote,

> They twisted even decent sin
> To shapes not to be named:
> Men were ashamed of honour;
> But we were not ashamed.

Gilbert just couldn't accept that evil didn't exist or that the honor of Horatius was something to be ashamed of. Gilbert didn't belong in this darkness. Was there a way out? Could G. K. Chesterton find his way out of this dark forest? No. The answer was simply, no. He would need someone to guide him.

Chapter Five

Gratitude and the Light

Gilbert was not thriving in art school. Fortunately, the University College also had literature classes, and Gilbert found himself shifting away from studying art and toward studying literature.

He also began revolting against the pessimistic skepticism that had engulfed him like a cloud. He began to reject the meaninglessness he perceived in the new philosophy of thought often associated with Impressionism. As he did, he began turning, slowly, toward God. This turn began with gratitude.

The words of his Puritan grandfather, his mother Ma-

rie-Louise's father, came to mind. Gilbert had never met him, but his mother had told him of a time when her aged father, who rarely spoke anymore, had surprised his family by suddenly interjecting into a discussion, "I should thank God for my creation if I knew I was a lost soul."

Gilbert began to be grateful. He wrote in his notebook:

> You say grace before meals.
> All right.
> But I say grace before the play and the opera,

And grace before the concert and
   pantomime,
And grace before I open a book,
And grace before sketching, painting,
Swimming, fencing, boxing, walking, playing,
   dancing;
And grace before I dip the pen in the ink.

It dawned upon Gilbert that there was someone who had given him all of these good things for which he could "say grace" and give prayers of thanksgiving.

He ought to thank God for creating him. Every day was a gift. God did exist. He was real. He was a personal God who gave these personal gifts. And what's more, Gilbert's existence, his life, had meaning because of it.

It was as if the forest mist had dissipated and the sun now shone a clear, life-giving light into G. K.'s world. The light lit up his path, showing him the way out of despair.

The new realization of gratitude became the path that led G. K. Chesterton to solid faith in God. He wrote in his notebook a few lines of verse, scrawling the title "Evening" above them.

> Here dies another day
> During which I have had eyes, ears, hands
> And the great world round me;
> And with tomorrow begins another.
> Why am I allowed two?

Life was an amazing gift. He was changed. No longer plagued with disturbing and anxious thoughts, no longer under a cloud, Gilbert felt a deep peace in his soul. He added to his notebook "The Prayer of a Man Resting."

> The twilight closes round me
> My head is bowed before the Universe
> I thank thee, O Lord, for a child I knew
>   seven years ago
> And whom I have never seen since.

He had turned to God in faith. He read the Bible. At some point during these years, he added these words to his notebook: "The right way is the Christian way." The gratitude he felt transformed his pessimism into optimism, and G. K. Chesterton began looking for the beauty and goodness in life. Finding goodness brought about a joy that most people noticed when they looked at him.

One May evening in 1895, the newly joyful Gilbert Keith Chesterton penned a letter to his lifelong friend Bentley. He wrote, "My joy in having begun my life is very great." He celebrated, "Being twenty-one years old is really rather good fun..." Gilbert was twenty-one years old, now officially a man. His future stretched out before him, looking bright and exciting.

He paused, looked up from his letter, and gazed out the window of his small apartment. In the street below, he saw a swarm of black hats, black coats, black trousers, and black umbrellas. The Londoners clad in all black were very "1895." The fashion trend reflected the mood of the late Victorian era in Britain. Black hats, black jackets, black trousers—black was the color of industry, of business. Depending on one's position in society, a man wore either a "frock coat," blue lounge suit, or "morning coat." Dark and uniform in color, the coat was a sign of the times.

Small touches of color were found in the neckties. Gentlemen wore top hats. These "stovepipes" or "chimney tops with a border" blended in with the dark chimney tops of

In the street below, he saw a swarm of black hats, black coats, black trousers, and black umbrellas.

the London skyline. If one was not a gentleman, he wore any of the dozens of styles of caps. As G. K. Chesterton studied the hats outside his window, he saw that many of the pedestrians were wearing the lower hats belonging to the office workers of society. The "Bowler" or "Coke" was a low, sturdy hat, made of pressed felt, with a rounded crown and a narrow brim. Though full, bushy beards had been common among Victorian men of the mid-century, now beards were beginning to look shorter. More men opted for the neatly-trimmed mustache.

Gilbert turned back to the letter he was writing to Bentley. The world was full of drab, colorless pessimism, but he had no room in his heart any longer for that feeling! He finished the letter, put his pen down, and stood to post it.

While studying literature at the University College, Gilbert met Ernest Hodder Williams, another student who recognized Gilbert's talent as a writer. Ernest's family was in the publishing business, and he asked Gilbert to write some book reviews for his family's publication, the *Bookman*. When Gilbert wrote the book reviews, he discovered his life pursuit. It wouldn't be drawing and painting; it would be writing.

Chapter Six

Mrs. Chesterton

G. K. Chesterton felt as if he stood at the threshold of the rest of his life. He had found his lifelong vocation; he would earn his living in publishing, journalism, and later, writing books. And yet something was still missing in his life. Gilbert wrote in his notebook.

Madonna Mia

About her whom I have not yet met
I wonder what she is doing
Now, at this sunset hour,
Working perhaps, or playing, worrying or laughing,

> Is she making tea, or singing a song, or writing,
> or praying, or reading
> Is she thoughtful, as I am thoughtful
> Is she looking now out of the window
> As I am looking out of the window?

Summer faded into autumn. Autumn brought crisp air and deep colors. No longer in school, Gilbert felt lonely. His friend Lucian had recently been smitten with a charming girl who lived in Bedford Park, a brand-new London suburb known for its artsiness. Indeed, Ethel Blogg had caught Lucian's eye in part because her family was popular in Bedford Park. Ethel's mother, Blanche Blogg, was a widow, which meant that Ethel and her two sisters, Gertrude and Frances, and brother Knollys were forced to find jobs and contribute to the family's support. Ethel and her sisters all worked as secretaries—Ethel for a group of doctors, Gertrude for the famous Rudyard Kipling (where she also was a governess for his children), and Frances for the Parents' National Education Union (P. N. E. U.).

The family was popular in the neighborhood partly because they were involved in a lively debating society called the I. D. K. One could immediately see the cleverness of this clan when learning the name of their debating society.

"The I. D. K.? What's that stand for?"

"I don't know."

"What do you mean, you don't know? You're a member aren't you?"

"Yes! That is why I'm telling you, 'I don't know!'"

It was hilarious.

One Saturday, Lucian said to Gilbert, "I am going to take you to see the Bloggs."

"The what?" asked Gilbert. It sounded like a pub. Lucian held him in suspense.

"The Bloggs. Let's go."

And they did. Lucian was glad to see Ethel again, but "The Bloggs" didn't seem all that remarkable to Gilbert. Still, he went along with Lucian a second time, and the second visit changed everything for him. As G. K. plopped down on the plush velvet furniture, he suddenly realized he was in the presence of an enchanting young lady. She was Ethel's sister, Frances.

Remembering himself, he stood and politely offered a greeting.

"It's a pleasure to meet you. My name is Gilbert Chesterton."

"Nice to meet you, Gilbert. I'm Frances."

The rest of that afternoon was somewhat of a blur to the young writer, though G. K. remembered vividly that she looked straight at him at one point with her soft, wise eyes. As she looked at him, he thought, "I ought to marry this girl." He was filled with a sense that Frances was honest and true and loyal. Gilbert was overcome. He

Gilbert was overcome. He described it later in a letter to Frances . . .

described it later in a letter to Frances: "Here ends my previous existence. Take it: it led me to you."

He started visiting the Blogg family each Sunday. He became the I. D. K. (I Don't Know) Debating Society's newest member on December 1, 1896. And he and Frances wrote letters to one another daily.

Charlotte Mason, the renowned British education re-

... *"Here ends my previous existence. Take it: it led me to you."*

former, had founded the P. N. E. U., where Frances worked. Miss Mason dedicated herself to providing educational resources to parents and teachers alike. "Children are born persons," Charlotte declared. In a time when children were often kept out of sight, brought up by governesses away in upstairs nurseries and then packed off to boarding school, it was almost revolutionary for her to remind parents of the individuality of their own children. The P. N. E. U. helped parents educate their young children at home.

The P. N. E. U. was located in Westminster. Frances took the sparkling, modern underground subway to work each day. Gilbert declined to travel in the "Tube," but he nevertheless would try to stop by Frances's workplace on his way to work in order to surprise her with a note or poem.

One evening, after Gilbert and Frances had each made their way home from a long day at work, Gilbert walked from Kensington to Bedford Park to call on Frances. He often stayed quite late and then walked home to Kensington in the midnight moonlight. On this particular evening, Frances had told Gilbert about her tiring day—so tiring that she had left her parasol at the train station. It was a minor thing, but on his way home that night, Gilbert passed by that same train station and remembered what Frances had told him. He suddenly decided to "commit his first and last crime," as he described it later. He crawled under the platform and squeezed into the station waiting area, spied Frances's parasol and snatched it up, leaving the same way he came in. Walking away in the dark, guilty yet triumphant, his top hat dented and his coat dirtied, it felt like he had fallen from the moon, with the parasol for a parachute.

On a beautiful day in July of 1898, Gilbert walked with his

Mrs. Chesterton

Gilbert knelt before her and asked for her hand in marriage.

love through St. James's Park in London. The sun soaked the park, shining on the lake where the ducks were happily gliding. As they crossed the St. James's bridge, Gilbert Keith Chesterton came to a stop in the middle and turned to his beloved Frances Alice Blogg. There he knelt before her and asked for her hand in marriage.

Frances happily accepted. They were engaged!

Gilbert was on top of the world with happiness. He

couldn't sleep that night, he was so overcome. He wrote to Frances.

> You will, I am sure, forgive one so recently appointed to the post of Emperor of Creation, for having had a great deal to do tonight before he had time to do the only thing worth doing. I have just dismissed with costs a case between two planets and am still keeping a comet (accused of furious driving) in the antechamber.

He felt like a king. It was truly as if he had never known happiness until now. He continued writing Frances,

> Happiness is not at all smug: it is not peaceful or contented, as I have always been until today. Happiness brings not peace but a sword; it shakes you like rattling dice; it breaks your speech and darkens your sight. Happiness is stronger than oneself and sets its palpable foot upon one's neck.

The two were engaged, but as events unfolded, their wedding wouldn't take place for three more years, much to their disappointment. The man who went on to write over one hundred books waited three years to marry his bride because he needed to earn enough money to support her.

The two spent as much time together as possible. They

often met in their beloved St. James's Park to read books together. When they weren't together, they wrote letters to one another. Gilbert wrote poems to his love. And Frances was known to press into books her favorite flowers—forget-me-nots and pansies—to give to Gilbert. The forget-me-nots symbolized that he was forever in her memory; the pansies symbolized that he was always in her thoughts.

In letters, Gilbert dreamed of their future home together. "When we set up a house, darling (honeysuckle porch, yew clipt hedge, bees, poetry and eight shillings a week), I think you will have to do the shopping." How well he knew that if it were up to him, they would only have chocolate-creams in the cupboard—all luxury, no necessities.

In the year following their engagement, tragedy struck Frances's family. Her beloved sister Gertrude, the sister who had worked for Rudyard Kipling and his family, was struck by a carriage as she rode on her bicycle and was killed. It was a shocking accident. The entire Blogg family felt deep sorrow. This sorrow sent Mrs. Blanche Blogg, Frances's mother, into a depression. Frances was also deeply grieved, and for a time, Gilbert worried that she might never recover from the sadness and depression. It took a while, but Frances found hope in the character of God. He is a good God, she knew, and she came to accept His will, even though it meant losing Gertrude.

At the dawn of a new century, Gilbert found a career opportunity as a journalist. He took a position as a writer for *The Speaker* publication. He contributed to the paper, which was a weekly review of London politics, literature, science, and the arts. This new job allowed him to bring home more money, which would be enough to support both him and Frances once they married.

In the year 1900, Gilbert managed to publish his first two books. *Greybeards at Play* was a collection of four whimsical rhymes with humorous illustrations drawn by Gilbert himself. He gave the second rhyme the title, "Of the Dangers Attending Altruism on the High Seas." The poem began with,

> Observe these Pirates bold and gay,
> That sail a gory sea:
> Notice their bright expression–
> The handsome one is me.

The pirates unfortunately encounter a pouring rain, in which they take pity on a fish they spy in the water, worrying that the poor thing has no way to stay dry. They absurdly take the fish onboard, where the fish suffered until they court-martialed him for his ungratefulness and sentenced him by throwing him back into the sea. It's an absurd and silly tale, ending with the moral:

> But—if you find a fish on land,
> Oh throw it in the sea.

Gilbert was as funny as ever.

The Wild Knight was also a collection of poems, including "The Donkey," a poem about the lowly donkey that carried Christ on Palm Sunday.

> When fishes flew and forests walked
>   And figs grew upon thorn,
> Some moment when the moon was blood
>   Then surely I was born.
>
> With monstrous head and sickening cry
>   And ears like errant wings,
> The devil's walking parody
>   On all four-footed things.
>
> The tattered outlaw of the earth,
>   Of ancient crooked will;
> Starve, scourge, deride me: I am dumb,
>   I keep my secret still.

> Fools! For I also had my hour;
>   One far fierce hour and sweet:
> There was a shout about my ears,
>   And palms before my feet.

Gilbert knew how much he owed to Frances and her encouragement for his writing success! He held a fresh copy of *The Wild Knight* tightly in his hands, then he proceeded to open it to the title page. Smiling, he thought back to how she had stood by him during the long journey of publishing. Overcome by a feeling of gratitude, he began writing a poem to his Frances. This is what Gilbert wrote:

> They love (the bonfire and sparks and stars)
> They fight (the war)
> She wards off the press
> He loves her like a princess
> She's all the world to him
> She takes sorrow in, and doesn't let it out
> She is wise
> (They are engaged but not yet married)

As he wrote that last line of poetry, Gilbert winced and managed a sigh. Couldn't they hurry up and have the wedding now, in April? Alas, the waiting was killing him! Although his books were well-received, the royalties were unremarkable, so Gilbert and Frances continued to wait.

Another year crawled by. Finally it was June 28, 1901. Two special occasions for celebration belonged to this day: Frances's thirty-second birthday and, at last, her wedding day!

Everyone gathered at St. Mary Abbots in Kensington for the long-anticipated wedding. Everything seemed to be in place, except—where was Gilbert's tie?

"Oh, dear!" Mrs. Blanche Blogg tried unsuccessfully to hold back a disconcerted grimace.

"Classic Gilbert!" mother of the groom, Marie-Louise Chesterton, giggled.

"Fetch Charles!" Mrs. Blogg looked around for Frances's young cousin. "Charles dear, there you are. Run and buy a tie for Gilbert! Thank you, dear boy. Now, hurry along!"

Off Charles ran. Ten minutes later, with the new tie in hand, he ran back through the neighborhood until he arrived at Kensington Church Street. He turned left and kept running. At this point, Charles could see the towering steeple of St. Mary Abbots. He ran under the Gothic arch that framed the doorway of the church and bolted to Gilbert. He held out the bow tie, a proud smile on his face.

Gilbert was as happy as a lark! He felt as if he were floating on a cloud as he greeted his bride at the altar. During the ceremony, as the couple knelt before Father Conrad Noel, Marie-Louise noticed something. Trying to hold back another giggle, she looked to the woman seated beside her, an old family friend named Annie. Pointing discreetly at Gilbert, Marie-Louise Chesterton supressed laughter. There, on the underside of Gilbert's shoe, was a forgotten price tag! Both Annie and Marie-Louise shared the knowledge that Frances would soon face a very difficult job: the job of keeping Gilbert presentable and punctual.

The marriage ceremony marked the beginning of a new chapter in Gilbert and Frances's life together. After they were pronounced husband and wife, Frances looked up at Gilbert, her new husband. Gilbert stood slender and tall on this special day. His wavy hair framed a face that appeared determined, yet content.

Catching her admiring gaze, G. K. returned it and in a cheerful tone remarked, "Frances, this is the day. After writing each other many letters, we have finally gotten married." As he said this, his mouth turned up in a warm smile.

Then his eyes became thoughtful-looking. He said in a contented yet serious tone, "Posting a letter and getting married are among the few things left that are entirely romantic; for to be entirely romantic, a thing must be irrevocable." Gilbert was thrilled to be Frances's husband for the rest of his life. He was entirely committed to her.

Mr. and Mrs. G. K. Chesterton walked through the majestic church doorway, hand-in-hand. There they greeted their family and close friends. Lucian Oldershaw was standing among them. He reminded Gilbert that the train for Ipswich was leaving the Liverpool Street station in just two hours.

"Yes, Lucian! Please take our bags to the train. I want to take Frances on a brief errand before we board." Lucian headed for the train station with the luggage.

The couple planned to travel to Norfolk Broads for their honeymoon but were to spend their first night at the White Horse Inn in Ipswich. But first, Gilbert Keith Chesterton had two important stops. He ran with his new wife to celebrate their nuptials with a glass of milk at the same dairy he had frequented as a child with his mother. Next, the couple stopped at another shop to buy a revolver—with cartridges. Then, almost skipping, with Frances

Then, almost skipping, with Frances beside him, Gilbert rushed to the train station.

beside him, Gilbert rushed to the train station.

Why would one buy a revolver on the way to his own honeymoon? To protect his bride! Gilbert later said, with a twinkle in his eye, that he wanted to protect Frances from "the pirates doubtless infesting the Norfolk Broads," as he put it.

The happy couple rushed to the station, but unfortunately they had missed their train. Off went the train, and off went their luggage! Laughing, they caught the slow train to Ipswich and the White Horse Inn.

The newlyweds spent their honeymoon amid the Norfolk Broads' shallow lakes, lush marshes, and vast woodlands. Gilbert had his revolver, laughter, and gratitude. Most importantly, he had his wife. The two were now a family. Family was important to G. K., and he believed it was one of God's ways to shower the world in grace.

Nonetheless, Frances had her hands full. During their engagement, she had gone on a "crusade of tidiness" as Gilbert put it. Combing his wild hair was no easy task. She loved him, but that hair! She tried, but it was a lost cause. One year into their marriage, Frances gave up fighting the unyielding force of nature that was Gilbert's hair.

"A hat will do the job of concealing the disheveled mane," Frances smiled with satisfaction as she placed a felt hat atop Gilbert's tall head, handed him a rather large cape coat, and finished off the ensemble by passing him his favorite swordstick.

This was Gilbert Keith Chesterton, ready to stand for truth and tradition against the forces of modernity, proud to have Frances by his side.

Chapter Seven

Man of Ideas

Gilbert took his stand against the forces of modernity from the area of London known as Fleet Street. Fleet Street was home to the publishing houses of England, and Gilbert's sword was his pen. He amazed his readers by weighing in on all sorts of topics—politics, religion, literature, and the arts. He artfully put his ideas into the written word, and his readers were captivated, even if they weren't always persuaded.

By 1902, G. K. was known for his essays. An essay is a writing composition that attempts to explain a particular subject and give an opinion or point-of-view about it. The word "essay" came to English from the French *essai*, which means "to test." The French word came from the Latin *exigere*, which means "to ascertain," or "to weigh." G. K. was able to take an idea and weigh it, in a sense. He examined all angles, arguments, and properties of his ideas. In this way, G. K. Chesterton defended truth and tradition against the attacks of modernity, just like the hero Horatius nobly fought to protect his beloved town from the enemy.

About this time, Gilbert seized on an idea for a novel.

They would fight for Notting Hill!

He got to thinking about how people imagined the most outrageous things about the future; or wondered what life would be like in one hundred years. Usually, people predicted doom and disaster. But Gilbert noticed that things rarely unfold as any generation imagines. He started to think about his home neighborhoods in London. What could happen far into the future?

London—with its sprawling streets filled with pedestrians. London—with its omnibus carriages streaking through Piccadilly Circus. London—with its bowler hats and black coats. Kensington. Hammersmith. Notting Hill. Battersea. What might happen if the King in the distant future declared that each neighborhood of London was its own little fortified city, with its own city wall, city guard, banner, and coat-of-arms?

Gilbert put this idea into his book *The Napoleon of Notting Hill*. King Auberon enacts the charter, and the provosts of the London boroughs are given their colors.

All seems well, until the King becomes interested in building a boulevard connecting Hammersmith Broadway with Westbourne Grove—right through the heart of West Kensington, North Kensington, and Notting Hill. Much to everyone's dismay and surprise, the Provost of Notting Hill, Adam Wayne, objects. *Not through Notting Hill! Pump Street in Notting Hill will not be destroyed!*

Adam Wayne rallies the people of Notting Hill to arms! They would fight for Notting Hill!

They would fight for Pump Street, the heart of Notting Hill. They would fight for the grocer there. They would fight for the old curiosity shop, which was full of swords and blunderbusses. They would fight for the toy and paper shop, which was their press. They would fight for the chemist's shop with its brightly-colored medicines encased in glass jars, which provided healing. They would fight for the barber shop, which stood in the middle of it all.

Adam Wayne, the hero of Notting Hill, took seriously what King Auberon later called a joke. The King didn't really mean that the neighborhoods of London should go to war! It was a joke!

But it was not a joke for Adam Wayne! He fought for his beloved Notting Hill with deep patriotism and bravery, eager to defend the village from the march of modernity.

The Napoleon of Notting Hill was imaginative and silly, and yet its story of conflict between tradition and modernism, belief and unbelief, was well-received.

England began to take notice of G. K. Chesterton's writing. It seemed that everyone was inviting Gilbert to speak to their groups or write for their publication. In addition, America found out about the young essayist and novelist. A *New York Times* contributor wrote of Chesterton, "There is little doubt that he will be read."

"What a sense of humor!" they marveled.

"A gifted satirist," they remarked.

In just a few years, G. K. Chesterton had written a variety of works. He was famous.

Chesterton believed that modern ideas about what was important and true were wrong. It was as if modernism were a disease spreading through culture like a plague. This plague sought to wipe out the belief that there was absolute truth coming from God.

G. K. was troubled that modern thinkers couldn't define what was "good." There were plenty of moderns discussing "progress," "liberty," and "education." G. K. believed these discussions were merely dodges to avoid discussing what was "good." Modern people said it was good to *not* judge what was "good" or "right." These thinkers insisted that no one could really say what was good, right, or true."

He thought about the word *orthodox*, which came from the Latin words for "right" and "belief." He realized that people no longer thought it was important to be orthodox—in fact, they were glad to be heretics! A heretic is someone who does *not* hold orthodox beliefs! How could modern people doubt that something could be "good" or "right"?

Gilbert wrote about this topic in his next book, which he called *Heretics*. In this book, rather than telling a silly story to make his point as he did in *The Napoleon of Notting Hill*, Gilbert took on heresies—false beliefs—and argued against them in essay form.

He pointed out that it made no sense to talk about "progress," a popular idea, while also insisting that there are no moral ideals of right or wrong. After all, *progress* depends on moving in a direction, improving from a worse situation to a better one. "For progress by its very name indicates a direction," he wrote. "But it is precisely about the direction that we disagree." Gilbert thought that the modern belief in progress didn't square with the modern belief that no one could know for sure what was good. How can you progress toward a better world if you can't be sure what a better world would be?

Chapter by chapter in *Heretics*, Gilbert took on the heresies he saw around him, even devoting chapters to famous literary men of his day. He faulted the poet and writer Rudyard Kipling for prizing military-like discipline above all else. He faulted the playwright George Bernard Shaw for agreeing with the atheist Nietzsche. He faulted the science fiction writer H. G. Wells for his utopian fantasies. Wells didn't believe that humans were tainted by original sin. He imagined a world without patriotic national boundaries, and therefore, he said, a world without war. But Gilbert retorted,

> It does not seem to occur to him that, for a good many of us, if it were a world-state we should still make war on it to the end of

> the world. For if we admit that there must be varieties in art or opinion what sense is there in thinking there will not be varieties in government?

Gilbert was fond of finding apparent contradictions between one idea and another—a paradox—then examining the truth in those contradictions.

> The strong cannot be brave. Only the weak can be brave; and yet again, in practice, only those who can be brave can be trusted, in time of doubt, to be strong.

He wrote that the more hopeless the situation appeared to be, the more hopeful the man must be. Chesterton's clever observations like this one earned him the nickname "Prince of Paradox."

G. K. Chesterton believed that if something was good, it was worth fighting for. He attacked the heresies with his writing, just as he still loved to attack the dahlias in his garden with his swordstick.

After *Heretics* was published in 1905, Gilbert published a biography of Charles Dickens. Then, in 1908, he published a fiction detective novel. G. K. didn't expect this book to amount to much. He even said in an interview that the book wouldn't survive for a hundred years. But instead,

The Man Who Was Thursday: A Nightmare has become one of his best-known works! In it, poet Gabriel Syme seeks to uncover an anarchist plot being carried out by the Central Anarchist Council, a group of seven people, each one named for one of the seven days of the week. It's a story of double-crossing undercover agents and disguise, where

it's difficult to know who is on the side of right. Gilbert said later that the whole story is a "nightmare of things, not as they are, but as they seemed to the young half-pessimist" that he was in his youth. "I thought it would be fun to make the tearing away of menacing masks reveal benevolence."

He fought battles in his essays and books, but he also loved a lively debate over a drink at Ye Olde Cheshire Cheese pub on Fleet Street. Gilbert was not only known around Fleet Street by almost everyone for his clever writing but also for his love of food and drink and his absent-minded eccentricity. He was acquainted with well-known British literary types, such as Sir J. M. Barrie, the playwright who wrote *Peter Pan*. Gilbert and the writer Hilaire Belloc joined forces in debate so often that George Bernard Shaw called them "Chesterbelloc."

After he published *Heretics*, several of his friends and critics around Fleet Street challenged him to write a follow-up that didn't just poke holes in what *others* believe, but explained what *G. K. Chesterton* believed. One critic said, "I'll begin to worry about my philosophy when Mr. Chesteron has given us his."

A publisher asked him, "Well, if a man is not to believe in himself, what is he to believe?"

Gilbert considered it.

"I will go home and write a book in answer to that question."

He often began the day with a hearty breakfast of hard-boiled eggs, scones, and marmalade. Then, fortified, G. K. would sit at the breakfast table, take up his pen, and write. Chesterton wrote the answer to the publisher's question with a strong defense of his own views in his next book,

Orthodoxy. While *Heretics* challenged false ideas; *Orthodoxy* defended true ideas.

It was clear to G. K. Chesterton that the modern world was upside-down, and it was the spiritual things of God that were the right-side-up things. He wrote that Christianity begins with the doctrine of original sin, something moderns were increasingly pretending didn't exist.

"It's the only part of Christian theology that can be proved!" Gilbert thought it madness to deny the reality of sin, which was plain by the evil seen everywhere.

"Original sin" is a term to describe the fact that every human is born a sinner. Gilbert saw that the Christian explanation of every human's sinful nature fit with reality. In *Orthodoxy*, he wrote about the other religions that denied the existence of original sin. He wrote about eastern mysticism, ancient paganism, and modern philosophies. He wrote about his journey from unbelief to belief in Christ.

G. K. Chesterton knew the human pain that comes from the reality of sin and the deep hunger that humans feel for a relationship with the Creator and Savior. He saw that the only fix for the world had to come from outside of it, from God himself. Only Christian teaching accounted for the reality of human sin and provided a cure.

A stick might fit into a hole, or a stone into a hollow, by accident. But for a key to fit into a complex lock and unlock it, it must be the right key. Gilbert saw that the key that fit the lock of the sinful, fallen world that we all experience was Christian orthodoxy.

Only Christianity, thought Gilbert, accounts for both the fact that humans were the most marvelous of all creatures, "the chief of creatures," *and* "the chief of sinners." Only Christianity crowned humans with dignity like the rays of the sun or the plumes of a peacock, while also showing the smallness of humans because of their sin.

These were furious opposites, thought Gilbert. Paradoxes. Only Christianity kept them both. "One can hardly think too little of one's self," said the Prince of Paradox. "One can hardly think too much of one's soul."

Still at the breakfast table, he took a moment to stretch and take a break from his writing. He knew Christianity possessed a treasure, and he had unearthed it. While outsiders to the faith only saw rigid doctrines and disciplines, he had found the everlasting joy and abundant freedom that comes from knowing Christ. Christ was the cure for the disease of sin. Christ died in the place of sinners, but he did not stay dead. A risen Christ is the hope for all humans. G. K. knew that hope.

Chapter Eight

Joy and Suffering

A few years before *Orthodoxy* was published, Gilbert had walked over the Yorkshire moors with a new friend, Father John O'Connor. Gilbert had met Father O'Connor while visiting friends in Ilkley. It had been spring. The air had been fresh and had smelled of new beginnings. The green blanket of the moor had been occasionally interrupted by bushy clusters of violet heather. The two men had walked together and had talked about human nature. As Gilbert had listened to Father O'Connor talk, he had been startled to realize just how much a priest like Father O'Connor knew of the depravity and sin of humans. Far from being innocent and ignorant of evil, a priest who hears the confessions of countless parishoners knows of evil all too well. This had given Gilbert an idea. Wouldn't it be interesting to write a story about a priest who solved crimes?

Gilbert created a colorful character based on his friend Father O'Connor and called him Father Brown. The funny irony of a godly clergyman investigating crimes and catching criminals made Gilbert's detective stories a hit. *The Innocence of Father Brown* was published in 1911. Gilbert would later publish four more collections of Father Brown stories. People are still reading Father Brown stories, and Gilbert's detective has even inspired a television series!

The white horse of Uffington was pure white against the green hilltop in Oxfordshire.

Joy and Suffering

The same year that *The Innocence of Father Brown* was published, Gilbert finished and published what many consider his masterpiece, *The Ballad of the White Horse*. The white horse in all its glory was an image that G. K. Chesterton held fondly from his earliest memories. The faint childhood memory of a white horse was a symbol of all he held dear. He remembered the White Horse Inn where he and Frances spent their honeymoon. And he thought about the great and mysterious White Horse visible on the green hill at Uffington since ancient times. He wanted to use the white horse in his writing in some way.

England's King Alfred had always inspired Gilbert's imagination. Alfred the Great was king of Wessex one thousand years before, in the ninth century. At the time, Alfred's Anglo-Saxon people were threatened by the invasion of Guthrum, the Danish pagan king. The Christian King Alfred heroically defended his homeland against the pagan invaders. It was a clash of culture and religion, and G. K. thought the historical events of King Alfred's fight to protect and preserve Christian England was not unlike the battle underway in his own lifetime. This time, the enemy threatening England was not an invading army of Danes—it was modernism. G. K. loved all that King Alfred represented. He was noble and heroic, standing strong against the onslaught of the enemy. He decided to tell the story of Alfred's battle against Guthrum and the pagan Danes in a ballad to illustrate a larger battle between good and evil, Christian and pagan. He worked on the poem for four years.

Gilbert wanted to see the places he was writing about. Hiring a driver, he and Frances traveled to the land of King Alfred. They visited Glastonbury and the Isle of Athelney, both in southwest England. The latter was said to be the fortress hiding place of King Alfred the Great during the Battle of Edington, where he defeated what was called the Great Heathen Army. Although the historical battle likely occurred to the west of Uffington, Gilbert set the historical battle there. Why? Because of the mysterious white horse on the hillside. Gilbert was interested in writing a poetic legend of King Alfred rather than a historical account of Alfred.

The white horse of Uffington was pure white against the green hilltop in Oxfordshire. How did it get there? Nobody knows for certain. The delicate trenches depict the form of a horse. Upon observation, one can see where the top layer of soil and grass were removed, and the white, chalky limestone underneath was exposed. Visitors to Uffington could still see the white horse scoured into the hilltop, its figure having been maintained for thousands of years.

In Gilbert's *Ballad of the White Horse*, King Alfred fights his battle against Viking warriors on this same hill. Alfred's victory is not only a victory for the Anglo-Saxons, it is a victory for Christ. The defeated ruler of the Vikings, Guthrum, is converted to Christianity at the end of the battle.

The end of the battle does not bring the end of challenges for King Alfred. Viking invasions continue to threaten the land. Just as the weeds on the white horse must continually be cleaned away, so Alfred calls on his people to continually drive back the invaders. In the poem, Alfred urges the English to faithfully maintain the white horse, to scour it pure white, over and over.

> And though skies alter and empires melt,
> This word shall still be true:
> If we would have the horse of old,
> Scour ye the horse anew.

A few years after publishing the poem, on the occasion of America entering the Great War, Gilbert wrote, "Unless a man becomes the enemy of an evil, he will not even become its slave but rather its champion."

As he and Frances looked out over the white horse at Uffington, a clear conviction came upon Gilbert. He remembered a verse from Paul's letter to the Ephesians. Paul wrote,

> For we wrestle not against flesh and blood, but against principalities, against powers, against the rulers of the darkness of this world, against spiritual wickedness in high places (Ephesians 6:12).

This was the fight Gilbert fought. *The Ballad of the White Horse* was like an ode to England. Some Englishmen even memorized it. One of these was the noteworthy British author C.S. Lewis, who decades later went on to say, "Don't you like the way Chesterton takes hold of you in [*The Ballad of the White Horse*], shakes you, and makes you want to cry?"

Of all Gilbert's poems, the *Ballad* was Frances's favorite. In its dedication, he wrote:

> Take these; in memory of the hour
> We strayed a space from home
> And saw the smoke-hued hamlets, quaint
> With Westland king and Westland saint,
> And watched the western glory faint
> Along the road to Frome.

The Chestertons had moved out of London in 1909, not long after *Orthodoxy* had been published. Their new dream home was called Overroads. It was situated on Grove Road in Beaconsfield. It was a big move for Gilbert and Frances, coming from London's gray and bustling streets to the quiet market town nestled in the countryside. Overroads, with its English Tudor-style architecture, seemed like a fairy-tale cottage. So different from London and its Fleet Street, the house in Beaconsfield was a perfect place for Gilbert to write.

There was much joy for the couple in country life. Plus,

Frances saw to it that Gilbert had plenty of exercise and fresh air in their new place. Likewise, Gilbert saw to it that Frances had plenty of sunshine to help brighten her spirit. The gray London fog had a way of bringing her down to a sad state of mind.

The Chestertons experienced much joy, but life had also brought grief and disappointment. Not only had Frances's brother tragically died, but Frances was deeply grieved that she and Gilbert were unable to have children. For years now, they had hoped for a baby. Frances had even undergone dangerous surgeries to try to fix the problem. But in spite of their efforts, they never became parents.

One afternooon at Overroads, Frances looked out the window and saw the neighborhood boys and girls playing. Oh, how she loved children! It was sad not to have any of her own, but Frances had determined to love and care for the children of her friends and family. Overroads was bustling that day! The neighborhood picnic wound down, and a group of children bounded through the front door into Overroads and down the hall to the library of the Chesterton home. Frances followed them into the book-lined room where Gilbert sat. With Gilbert around, there was never a dull moment! He dropped down on all fours, rose up, and pawed the air with his front "legs." He let out a deafening ROAR! The children laughed. Meanwhile, two girls crossed the room to the sofa where Frances sat with her back to the antics. Frances opened up a book of fairy tales and began reading to them quietly.

All of a sudden, there was a loud *thud!* behind them. Frances sprang to her feet to see what was the matter and found that little Johnny had jumped on Gilbert and was trying to wrestle the large "lion." Gilbert, in full lion character, had collapsed to the ground and was feigning sleep. Giggles erupted from the young crowd of guests.

Frances fought the urge to roll her eyes. These antics! Gilbert Keith Chesterton was nothing more than a big child himself!

The Chestertons looked forward to their annual Christmas party for children. Frances's sister Ethel and her husband Lucian, Gilbert's old school friend, lived close by in Beaconsfield. Their daughter Catherine, affectionately called Kate, was very close with her Aunt Frances. Frances liked writing songs and even plays for the nieces and nephews to perform. She even wrote a song for Kate's school.

Gilbert and Frances were sad not to have their own children, but they loved many, many who belonged to others. They even became godparents—for twenty-five different children.

The year 1914 brought great change for the Chestertons and for all of Europe. On June 28, a Serbian nationalist assassinated Archduke Franz Ferdinand, heir to the Austro-Hungarian Empire. The Great War had begun.

Gilbert and Frances were sad not to have their own children, but they loved many, many who belonged to others.

By October of that year, Gilbert had developed a sniffle, then a cough. The lingering cough had resulted from exhaustion and taking on too many writing projects. But this wasn't merely a cold; by November, it was clear that Gilbert was very ill. The doctor pronounced heart trouble. Frances needed two additional nurses to help her care for Gilbert. He mostly kept to his bed and even drifted in and out of consciousness. In December, he seemed to be improving. Unfortunately, that Christmas Eve, after the carolers had gone home for the night and the town of Beaconsfield had gone to bed, Gilbert's condition took a terrible turn. Quickly, Frances called the nurses to help, and then summoned the town doctor, who came at once. After a thorough examination, the doctor concluded that Gilbert's heart was dangerously weak and had caused the attack.

Frances worried. Would Gilbert survive? No one could say. Following the medical advice of the day, he was kept unconscious much of the time. Frances and the nurses could only care for him as best they could—and pray.

Frances feared that she would lose her beloved. The days crawled by, and Gilbert hung on to life. Frances decided to gather together some of Gilbert's poems and publish them in a collection. She added a few of the love poems he had written to her, eager for the world to know the loving man she adored.

She sat flipping through the many love poems Gilbert had written for her. Keeping the most personal poems to her-

She sat flipping through the many love poems Gilbert had written for her.

self, she selected some that she wanted to share with the world. Seeing his precious words on the page brought her to tears. Gilbert was everything to her! Bowing her head and closing her tear-filled eyes, Frances prayed silently for God to heal her husband.

In January 1915, it seemed as if he was turning a corner in his recovery. Lying in bed, he opened his eyes and started speaking clearly. He called out to Frances, who was darning socks in her favorite seat by the kitchen fireplace.

Immediately, she came running to his room, and the two embraced each other in a hug. Cupping his face in her hands, Frances began to cry tears of relief and gratitude. His eyes and smile looked weak, but he was the same Gilbert. That glimpse of his recovery was enough to keep Frances going until he fully recovered. It was slow going, but that Easter, Gilbert was back on his feet. Frances felt the timing was no accident. Gilbert's recovery felt to her almost like a resurrection.

Frances rejoiced at God's gracious healing power. The playful lion was back again, ready to write in full force.

Chapter Nine

Patience

In the spring of 1915, G. K. Chesterton sat upright in bed and thanked God for the beginning of his healing. After his return to work, he wrote with a renewed vigor and pace. It was not uncommon for G. K. to be writing multiple books or articles at once.

"You have so many irons in the fire," many of his friends commented. It hadn't taken too long to bounce back. There was plenty of mail from his readers to prove it! He dedicated the next couple of years to fully recovering from the illness and writing.

The war in Europe dragged on, and in 1916, G. K.'s

brother Cecil joined the army. Cecil married Ada Jones, a journalist sometimes called the "Queen of Fleet Street." After a brief honeymoon, Cecil left England for the front lines. He was wounded three times fighting in France. Surviving those events, he later became ill with kidney disease and died in a field hospital, just one month after the Armistice, in December 1918. Gilbert mourned the loss of his brother. He would have to be patient, as he longed to see him again in heaven.

In the years following the end of the Great War, Gilbert began traveling abroad. He was well known by this time and received many invitations to speak or lecture. In 1918, he lectured in Ireland. The next year he made a trip to Palestine and on his way to Jerusalem went through Paris, Rome, Alexandria, and Cairo. This trip inspired his book *The New Jerusalem*.

In January 1921, Gilbert and Frances climbed aboard a ship headed for America, after receiving his doctor's clearance. This tour would permit the couple to see America while receiving payment for speaking engagements. Their itinerary in America would take them to many places: New York, Albany, Boston, Chicago, Philadelphia, Baltimore, Nashville, Oklahoma, Omaha, and, in Canada, Toronto, Ottawa, and Montreal.

The crowds in New York were eagerly preparing for their arrival from across the ocean. Frances and Gilbert

Frances and Gilbert marveled at New York's growing skyline from their approaching ocean liner.

marveled at New York's growing skyline from their approaching ocean liner. The tall buildings seemed to have spotted them from a distance and alerted all of New York's reporters, because an overwhelming throng of people greeted the Chestertons at the port. Frances especially was overwhelmed. As the steamship docked, reporters on shore shouted questions to the couple.

Gilbert and Frances were taken aback by all the fuss. It almost took her breath away when a reporter asked Frances for an interview! Partially flattered, partially on-edge, Frances did her best to answer the reporter's questions. She answered as many questions as she could, one by one.

Along with Gilbert's many speaking engagements, the couple connected with old friends from home who were now in America. They caught up with neighbors from their time in Battersea, and saw a former pupil of Lucian Oldershaw's. Frances had lunch with Aline Kilmer, the widow of poet Joyce Kilmer, who had been killed in the war.

The Chestertons enjoyed almost four months in America, but in April of 1921 they were very glad to return to their home Overroads in Beaconsfield, outside of London. Gilbert wrote about their trip in *What I Saw in America*, which was published the following year.

With the soft caress of springtime in Beaconsfield, the Chestertons finally moved across the street to Top Meadow, their new home. Many years earlier in 1913, Gilbert and Frances had admired the property across the street from their rented home Overroads. They had used profits from the success of the Father Brown books to purchase the land and had begun building a writing studio for Gilbert. After the studio had been completed, they had added their home onto the studio. Top Meadow was an estate resembling their Overroads home with its Tudor style.

The gardens of Top Meadow were a sight and smell to behold! The south-facing bow window in the new home overlooked the gardens and a meadow. The south garden produced flowers of all colors while the north side of the house displayed hedges, lime, cherry, holly, and cypress trees. Frances especially enjoyed the fragrant gardens. The large kitchen vegetable garden was a sight too. From her flower beds, Frances picked bouquets of flowers. She found a new hobby in arranging them.

"Do you know the significance of this honeysuckle?" She quizzed Gilbert.

"Oh dear! I hope I can remember the significance. Ah! It came from the plant cutting we rooted after we got married. Once it grew, we transplanted it at Overroads!" Gilbert smiled with satisfaction.

"And now I'm transplanting a cutting here at Top Meadow." Frances thought she could not be happier.

The next year brought both joy and sadness to Gilbert and Frances. Sadly, Mr. Ed, Gilbert's inventive father, died in the spring of 1922. Once again, G. K. did not mourn as one without hope. Just a few months later, Gilbert took a significant step in his spiritual journey. He became a Roman Catholic.

Gilbert had been drawn to the church's history and theology and for some time now had been moving toward conversion from his Protestant form of Christianity. On the day Gilbert became a Roman Catholic, the ceremony was held in an unlikely setting. On Sunday, July 30, his friend Father O'Connor and Father Rice met with Gil-

On Sunday, July 30, his friend Father O'Connor and Father Rice met with Gilbert and Frances . . .

bert and Frances in a makeshift church located in a tin shed at the back of the Railway Hotel. At any minute, a train could come chugging along the tracks and screech to a halt, drowning out the priests' voices! It was an unlikely place for his conversion ceremony, but that didn't matter. Frances, although in great pain from her now failing health, attended the ceremony. Four years later, Frances would also convert to Roman Catholicism.

Gilbert continued his life of thinking, writing, and lecturing. In 1925, after his friend and intellectual rival H. G. Wells wrote his atheistic *Outline of History*, Gilbert Keith Chesterton sat down in his study to respond with what would become his most important book, *The Everlasting Man*. Years into the future, this book would impact a man by the name of C. S. Lewis. When Lewis later wrote about his spiritual conversion from atheism to Christianity in *Surprised by Joy*, he mentioned Chesterton's *The Everlasting Man* as being influential for him. Chesterton continued to insist in his lectures and writings that the modern denial of God didn't make sense.

To defend his point as an apologist was no easy feat, but G. K. had the patience, the wit, and the Christian gratitude to press on towards the truth. Chesterton's goal was not to degrade or defame his opponents. It was rather to persuade them with the "Man with the Golden Key" message of Christian charity.

Who was this Man with the Golden Key? Chesterton

wanted everyone to know that Christ himself was the everlasting Man, the Man with the Golden Key.

"Frances! Would you please listen to this revision? I think you'll like it, dear. Do you remember the little toy theater Mr. Ed made? The one with the man who held a golden key? Well, I've been thinking about him a lot."

Gilbert reminded Frances of the time in art school when he had become lost in the murky forest of his mind. He had searched for light amid the tangled branches. When the mist had dissipated and light had finally shone clearly, it had settled on the Man with the Golden Key.

Looking back, Gilbert could see now that it was the Man with the Golden Key who had beckoned him. The bridge had already been built. All he had to do was take a step out of the forest and onto the bridge, toward the Man with the Golden Key, Jesus Christ.

Once he had stepped into the faith, he had become more and more aware of his own sin and his need for the Man. Every day, he had a new need to keep the Man in his sight. He knew the Man delighted in him. He knew he had assurance of his position, that he was no longer His enemy, but he was forgiven. As he had continued his journey, he had reached the Man with the Golden Key. Light shone from His face and reflected off of G. K.'s face. He had to turn away, it was so bright!

This light not only lit up his face in great radiance; it ignited a fire in his heart that illuminated the answer to the riddle of life. This Man gave him clear instructions in His book about how to love his enemies, how to speak to his opponents, and how to embrace orthodox thinking. He encouraged Gilbert to abide in Him, as He abided in Gilbert.

Gilbert reminded Frances of how, with the Man's help, he aimed to slow the spread of the disease of unorthodox thinking through his books, *Heretics* and *Orthodoxy*. Only Christ, the Man with the Golden Key, was the cure for the disease of sin. Not only that, but his key also unlocked the answer to the riddle of life.

When G. K. had been writing his conclusion to *The Everlasting Man,* he paused to share a passage with Frances, who was by his side.

> [Christendom] is the one mind that remains unbroken in the break-up of the world. If it were an error, it seems as if the error could hardly have lasted a day. If it were a mere ecstasy, it would seem that such an ecstasy could not endure for an hour. It has endured for nearly two-thousand years; and the world within it has been more lucid, more level-headed, more reasonable in its hopes, more healthy in its instincts, more humorous and cheerful in the face of fate and death, than all the world outside.

Top Meadow

"How does that read, Frances?"

Frances nodded and smiled a little. Her patient, wise eyes reflected a love for her husband. There was a lot to love in Gilbert, as anyone could plainly see. But Frances had weathered the storms of life with him and had become a more joyful and wonder-filled person because of him.

You see, Gilbert Keith Chesterton exuded joy. He loved vibrantly and with joy. His blotting pads were decorated with copious sketches of knights in shining armor, caricatures that would make children laugh and beg for more.

He wrote poetry and spoke his own love-filled life into his poems. He lived life in wonder. His work required young atheists to think. His wit and humor moved would-be enemies to acquiesce to friendship.

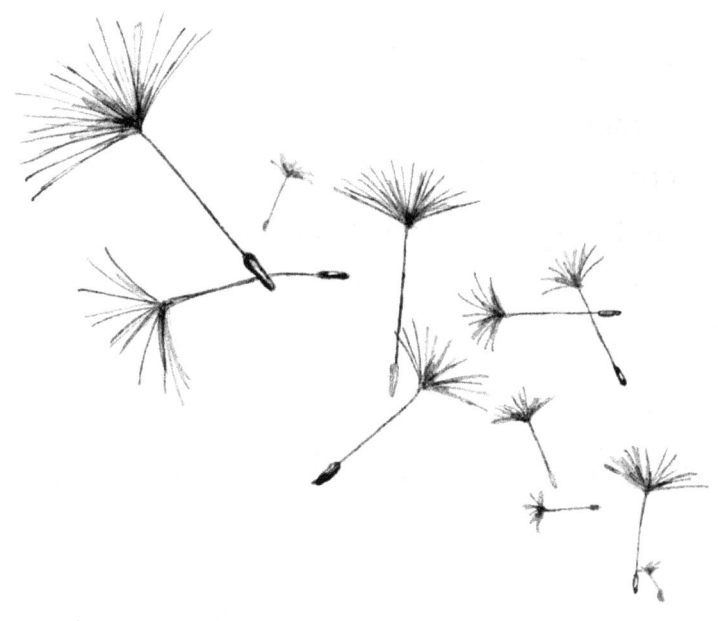

Chapter Ten

Stepping out into the Light

A dandelion seed floated like a parachute over the bench where G. K. Chesterton sat at the Market Harborough train station. Upon seeing it, he chuckled and remarked, "How wonderful!" As he gathered his writings to head back to Top Meadow for a meal with Frances, he checked on her telegram. She told him exactly where he should be, as usual. Stepping out into the light of the setting sun, he walked towards the ticket office. He recalled the man with the golden key in his father's toy theater. That man had been walking across the bridge to save his princess. Yet, G. K. Chesterton knew that,

> He who is called Pontifex, the Builder of the Bridge, is called also Claviger, the Bearer of the Key; and that such keys were given him to bind and loose when he was a poor fisher in a far province, beside a small and almost secret sea.

His faith in the Man with the Golden Key, Jesus Christ, was strong. Smiling, he boarded his train and headed home.

Ever grateful, G. K. Chesterton urged others toward a life of confession and gratitude. In his writings, he revealed that the "chief idea of his life" was to be filled with gratitude for all things. He reminded others that Christian doctrine begins with acknowledgement of original sin. Only knowing the depth of sin and evil's corruption of humanity could prepare one to understand one's need for salvation. Confessing one's sin and turning towards the forgiveness Christ offers brings new life. One can only respond to the grace of God, who gives all good things including salvation, with gratitude and wonder.

"It is not familiarity but comparison that breeds contempt," G. K. wrote. Where there was gratitude, there was no comparison. Using dandelions as an example, G. K. explained how one person might grumble at the "weed," showing great contempt. Another person might whine,

"Shall we feel no wonder at them at all, and above all no wonder at being thought worthy to receive them?"

"you can get better dandelions elsewhere."

"Did these people not understand that we humans have no right to dandelions? Shall we feel no wonder at them at all, and above all no wonder at being thought worthy to receive them?" G. K. wondered in his autobiography.

Chesterton spent the last years of his life traveling and speaking, wanting all who heard him to know the Truth. He sought to challenge the prevailing modern ideas that denied God and left people without hope. His many trips took him and Frances to Spain, Poland, Belgium, Rome, and again to America. In Rome in 1929, he met Pope Pius XI and also Benito Mussolini. In America, he lectured at the University of Notre Dame, Milwaukee, Chicago, Detroit, and, in Canada, Toronto, Quebec, and Montreal. He and Frances concluded this trip on the east coast of the United States, in Massachusetts and New York City.

In 1933, both Frances and Gilbert mourned the death of their mothers. Gilbert himself was suffering from increasingly poor health. He made some more trips around Europe, including one to the south of France in May of 1936 in the hope that the climate would improve his health. He published his *Autobiography* in January of that year, as it turned out, just before the end of his life.

Gilbert Keith Chesterton died on June 14, 1936. The Prince of Paradox had gone to be with his Savior, the Man with the Golden Key. Hearing the news of his lifelong friend's death, E. C. Bentley wrote:

> A giant of English letters ... has been taken from us... With Gilbert Chesterton gone, the world can never be the same again."

Author's Note

Anyone acquainted with G. K. Chesterton's work can testify that he was unique. He was one of the few of his time to still relish the classical medieval tradition. He was a man of ideas and could elaborate on one point for many pages. His work spanned the broad landscape of literature, as he became an avid essayist, poet, novelist, journalist, apologist, and playwright. Even more importantly, his life embodied a pursuit of joy and virtue, ultimately, in pursuit of His Lord and Savior, Jesus Christ.

In well-known C.S. Lewis's *Abolition of Man*, he writes about the dehumanizing effect of our modern education system. The transcendent virtues of truth, goodness, and beauty have been cut out of a modern education. In effect, people are forgetting the answer to this question: "What is it to be human?"

Lewis was one of G. K. Chesterton's protégés. Even though the two never spent time together, Lewis cited many of G. K. Chesterton's works that influenced his own thinking. G. K. Chesterton's *The Everlasting Man* was one of the catalysts in Lewis's conversion to Christianity. Lewis states:

> Then I read Chesterton's *Everlasting Man* and for the first time saw the whole Christian outline of history set out in a form that seemed to make sense.

There is nothing too surprising in G. K. Chesterton's belief in God's goodness and common grace extended to people in everything from the rain shower to the dandelion "weed," as seen in this story.

C.S. Lewis might have been called a "lion for truth," but G. K. Chesterton was a defender of truth, as well. From Chesterton's very first memory of the toy theater, to the white horse, to the beauty found in family and ordinary life, he looked to find beauty and meaning in nearly everything. His conversion to Christianity was a defining moment in his life, as he began to see the truth and feel a great sense of gratitude for his life.

His supportive and loving wife was herself a defender of an education that upholds and embraces ideas of virtue, having worked closely with education reformer Charlotte Mason. Frances Blogg Chesterton was indeed a gem. She was the steady rock in the family who made sure G. K. knew where he needed to be and at what time he needed to arrive.

G. K. Chesterton was a thinker, a debater. However, his humility and self-deprecating humor set him apart from others. He had a respect for the virtue found in an opponent. Even some of his staunchest opponents were also self-described friends (*i.e.*, H.G. Wells and G. B. Shaw).

This story is my attempt to communicate and to celebrate the basic virtues G. K. Chesterton pursued, to convey his joy and wisdom, and to explain how he became the man whose name so many people have come to love and revere. I also highlight the relationship between G. K. and his wife, Frances. Their joy in suffering underscores the great patience they displayed throughout their lives.

The Life of Chesterton: The Man Who Carried a Swordstick and a Pen brings the person of G. K. Chesterton to life for readers. May you find noble ideas in his noble ideas. May you find virtue in his life, words, and actions. Above all, I pray these things point you to Jesus.

Holly Geiger Lee

Bibliography

Belmonte, K.C. *Defiant Joy: The Remarkable Life and Impact of G. K. Chesterton*. Nashville: Thomas Nelson, 2011.

Brown, Nancy Carpenter. *The Woman Who Was Chesterton*. The American Chesterton Society, 2015.

Chesterton, Ada Elizabeth. *The Chestertons*. London: Chapman & Hall, Ltd, 1941.

Chesterton, G. K., and Randall Paine. *The Autobiography of G.K. Chesterton*. San Francisco, Calif: Ignatius Press, 2006.

Chesterton, G. K. *The Everlasting Man*. New York: Dodd, Mead, and Company, 1925.

Chesterton, G. K. *Greybeards at Play: Literature and Art for Old Gentlemen*. London: R. Brimley Johnson, 1900.

Chesterton, G. K. *Heretics*. New York: John Lane Company, 1919.

Chesterton, G. K. *The Man Who Was Thursday: A Nightmare*. New York: Dodd, Mead and Company, 1908.

Chesterton, G. K. *Orthodoxy*. New York: Dodd, Mead, and Company, 1927.

Chesterton, G. K. *The Wild Knight and Other Poems*. London: Grant Richards, 1900.

Coren, Michael. *Gilbert: The Man Who Was G. K. Chesterton*. Jonathan Cape, Ltd, 1989. Lume Books, 2018. Kindle.

Gilbert, W. S. *The Bab Ballads*. London: Macmillan & Co Ltd, 1904.

Lewis, C. S. *Surprised by Joy: The Shape of My Early Life*. Harcourt Brace, 1984.

Oddie, William. *Chesterton and the Romance of Orthodoxy: The Making of GKC, 1874-1908*. Oxford: Oxford University Press, 2008.

Sayer, George. *Jack: A Life of C. S. Lewis*. Wheaton, Ill: Crosswway Books, 1988.

Ward, Maisie. *Gilbert Keith Chesterton*. New York: Sheed & Ward, 1943. Aeterna Press, 2014. Kindle.

Acknowledgements

My deepest thanks goes out to all who helped me work on this project. To Amy Edwards and Tina Mugglin, the wonderful team at Blue Sky Daisies: I could not have proceeded on this project without your support.

To Nellie Buchanan, an artist who has a true ability to capture the simple joy of a nostalgic era, with her vintage art: you made this project come to life.

To the people who have answered my research questions, namely, Vicar Timothy Thompson: your first hand perspective is so valuable and helped me immensely in making this project.

To my friends who have supported me near and far, you know who you are: the homeschooling "mompreneurs" who have given me a platform to talk about my project, who have shared opportunity after opportunity with me, who have encouraged me and given me great advice: Amy Sloan, Laura McKinney Adams, Melissa Brander, and Sara Jordan, thank you so much!

To my local friends in the city of Wilson: you all are a supportive group of neighbors. I am so glad to live, work, and play around you.

To my extended family members, who have offered so much encouragement and support: Winston Brady of Thales Academy, thank you for the podcast interviews and feedback.

And of course, to my husband and children: Andrew, Nathanael, Virginia, and Connor. Thank you for giving me the gift of time: time to pursue this project, and time with you, which is ever so much more special to me. I love you so much!

Thank you to the One who gives me the ability to breathe right now, as well as type this message. You've given me eyes to see that You hold the key to everything. Thank you Jesus. To You be the glory forever and ever.

Endnotes

18 *"I was the mother of three children," she had said:* Ada Elizabeth Chesterton, *The Chestertons* (London: Chapman & Hall, Ltd, 1941), 22.
32 *...he sent Bentley a letter:* William Oddie, *Chesterton and the Romance of Orthodoxy: The Making of GKC, 1874-1908* (Oxford: Oxford University Press, 2008), 46
39 *"Our debating club was actually founded":* G. K. Chesterton, *The Autobiography of G. K. Chesterton* (San Francisco, Calif: Ignatius Press, 2006), 68.
40 *"The dragon is certainly":* Michael Coren, *Gilbert: The Man Who Was G. K. Chesterton* (Jonathan Cape, Ltd, 1989. Lume Books, 2018. Kindle), 41.
41 *"I'm a Member, I'm a Member":* Michael Coren, *Gilbert: The Man Who Was G. K. Chesterton* (Jonathan Cape, Ltd, 1989. Lume Books, 2018. Kindle), 46.
42 *"Six feet of genius":* Michael Coren, *Gilbert: The Man Who Was G. K. Chesterton* (Jonathan Cape, Ltd, 1989. Lume Books, 2018. Kindle), 48.
44 *"An Idyll":* Michael Coren, *Gilbert: The Man Who Was G. K. Chesterton* (Jonathan Cape, Ltd, 1989. Lume Books, 2018. Kindle), 55.
46 *"I was simply carrying the skepticism...":* G. K. Chesterton, *The Autobiography of G. K. Chesterton* (San Francisco, Calif: Ignatius Press, 2006), 97.
49 *"A cloud was on the minds of men":* G. K. Chesterton, *The Man Who Was Thursday: A Nightmare* (New York: Dodd, Mead and Company, 1908), iv.
52 *"I should thank God for my creation":* G. K. Chesterton, *The Autobiography of G. K. Chesterton* (San Francisco, Calif: Ignatius Press, 2006), 29.
52 *"You say grace before meals":* Michael Coren, *Gilbert: The Man Who Was G. K. Chesterton* (Jonathan Cape, Ltd, 1989. Lume Books, 2018. Kindle), 74.
54 *"Here dies another day":* Maisie Ward, *Gilbert Keith Chesterton* (New York: Sheed & Ward, 1943. Aeterna Press, 2014. Kindle), 58.
54 *"I thank thee, O Lord, for the stones in the street":* Maisie Ward, *Gilbert Keith Chesterton* (New York: Sheed & Ward, 1943. Aeterna Press, 2014. Kindle), 59.
55 *"The right way is the Christian way":* Michael Coren, *Gilbert: The Man Who Was G. K. Chesterton* (Jonathan Cape, Ltd, 1989. Lume Books, 2018. Kindle), 74.
59 *"Madonna Mia":* Maisie Ward, *Gilbert Keith Chesterton* (New York: Sheed & Ward, 1943. Aeterna Press, 2014. Kindle), 77.
62 *"Here ends my previous existence":* Maisie Ward, *Gilbert Keith Chesterton* (New York: Sheed & Ward, 1943. Aeterna Press, 2014. Kindle), 92.
66 *"You will, I am sure, forgive me":* Michael Coren, *Gilbert: The Man Who Was G. K. Chesterton* (Jonathan Cape, Ltd, 1989. Lume Books, 2018. Kindle), 100.
70 *"They love (the bonfire and sparks and stars)":* Nancy Carpenter Brown, *The Woman Who Was Chesterton* (The American Chesterton Society, 2015), 45.
94 *"Don't you like the way":* George Sayer, *Jack: A Life of C.S. Lewis* (Wheaton, Ill.: Crossway Books, 1988), xix.
109 *"[Christendom] is the one mind that remains unbroken":* G. K. Chesterton, *The Everlasting Man* (New York: Dodd, Mead and Company), 340.
114 *"But I know that he who is called Pontifex":* G. K. Chesterton, *The Autobiography of G. K. Chesterton* (San Francisco, Calif: Ignatius Press, 2006).
114 *"chief idea of his life":* G. K. Chesterton, *The Autobiography of G. K. Chesterton* (San Francisco, Calif: Ignatius Press, 2006), 325.
114 *"It is not familiarity but comparison":* G. K. Chesterton, *The Autobiography of G. K. Chesterton* (San Francisco, Calif: Ignatius Press, 2006), 327.
116 *"A giant":* E. C. Bentley, *The Spectator*, 19 June 1936, p. 9. https://archive.spectator.co.uk/article/19th-june-1936/9/g-k-c. Accessed June 18, 2024.
117 *"Then I read":* C. S. Lewis, *Surprised by Joy* (New York: Harcourt Brace Jovanovich, 1956), 223.

HOLLY GEIGER LEE lives in her home of North Carolina, where she has worked in the fields of education and counseling. A homeschooling mother to three and wife to Andrew, Holly loves to read with her children, participate in family games, and take dance lessons with her husband. Her work at mylittlebrickschoolhouse.com connects parents and children with living books.

NELLIE BUCHANAN grew up along with her seven siblings in rural upstate New York not far from the small town of Owego. Ever since she was young, Nellie enjoyed capturing the scenes and emotions of life around her through her art. Her family lived in a 19th-century farmhouse and there were plenty of beautiful paintings, old books, and animals around to delight her imagination. As her talent developed, Nellie discovered and fell in love with the works of Norman Rockwell, N. C. Wyeth, and Robert McCloskey, among others. These artists not only captured the essence of the great romantic epic, but they also beautifully expressed the romance of the everyday commonplace, and were the driving influencers of her work. As William Osler put it so nicely, "Nothing will sustain you more potently than the power to recognize in your humdrum routine, as perhaps it may be thought, the true poetry of life."

More from Blue Sky Daisies

Cindy Rollins
Beyond Mere Motherhood: Moms Are People Too by Cindy Rollins
Morning Time: A Liturgy of Love by Cindy Rollins
The Morning Time Student Anthology by Cindy Rollins
Hallelujah: Cultivating Advent Traditions with Handel's Messiah by Cindy Rollins
The Literary Life Commonplace Books by Angelina Stanford, Cindy Rollins, and Thomas Banks
The Literary Life KIDS Commonplace Books by Angelina Stanford, Cindy Rollins, and Thomas Banks

Charlotte Mason
Charlotte Mason: The Teacher Who Revealed Worlds of Wonder by Lanaya Gore and illlustrated by Twila Farmer
The Charlotte Mason Book of Quotes: Copywork to Inspire by Lanaya Gore

Geography Books
Elementary Geography by Charlotte Mason
Home Geography for Primary Grades with Written and Oral Exercises by C. C. Long

Language Arts and Grammar Books
The Mother Tongue: Adapted for Modern Students by George Lyman Kittredge
　In this series: Text; Workbook 1 and 2; Answer Key 1 and 2
Exercises in Dictation by F. Peel
Grammar Land: Grammar in Fun for the Children of Schoolroom Shire (Annotated) by M. L. Nesbitt and annotated by Amy M. Edwards and Christina J. Mugglin

The CopyWorkBook Series
The CopyWorkBook: Writings of Charlotte Mason by Lanaya Gore
The CopyWorkBook: George Washington's Rules of Civility & Decent Behavior in Company and Conversation by Amy M. Edwards and Christina J. Mugglin
The CopyWorkBook: Comedies of William Shakespeare by Amy M. Edwards and Christina J. Mugglin

Other Titles
Umbrellas by Twila Farmer
The Birds' Christmas Carol by Kate Douglas Wiggin
The Innkeeper's Daughter by Michelle Lallement
Kipling's Rikki-Tikki-Tavi: A Children's Play by Amy M. Edwards

Coming Soon
Tell It Back! A Sunday School Curriculum with a Charlotte Mason Approach by Tracy Fast
Shakespeare's A Midsummer Night's Dream: Play On! Kids on Stage by Jenny Bradley
Shakespeare's A Midsummer Night's Dream Puppets by Sadie Noone

Visit BlueSkyDaisies.net for a complete list of Blue Sky Daisies books.

www.ingramcontent.com/pod-product-compliance
Lightning Source LLC
Chambersburg PA
CBHW070449050426
42451CB00015B/3405